Start Reading
AND **WRITING**

How Does it Grow?
Seed to Sunflower

Ian Smith

QED Publishing

First published in the UK in 2004 by
QED Publishing
A Quarto Group Company
226 City Road
London, EC1V 2TT

www.qed-publishing.co.uk

A Catalogue record for this book is available from the British Library.

ISBN 1 84538 318 4

Written by Ian Smith
Designed by Zeta Jones
Editor Hannah Ray
Picture Researcher Joanne Beardwell
Illustrated by Chris Davidson

Series Consultant Anne Faundez
Creative Director Louise Morley
Editorial Manager Jean Coppendale

Printed and bound in China

Picture credits
Key: t = top, b = bottom, m = middle, c = centre, l = left, r = right

Corbis/ Dennis Blachut 12,/ Becky Lulgart–Stayner 16,/ Owaki–Kulla 9,/ Tom
Stewart 8,/ Jim Sugar 14,/ Ron Watts 11; **Ecoscene**/ Papilio Robert Picket 6t, 6m,
6b, 7, 13; **Getty**/ Davies & Star 4m, 22t,/ John Lawrence 10,/ Rita Maas 4t,/ Steve
Satushek 5,/ Paul Vlant 17.

Contents

How does it grow? 4

Sunflower sizes 8

Flowers in bloom 10

Sunflower seeds 12

Growing again 14

Good to eat 16

How to grow a sunflower 18

Planting the seedlings 20

Glossary 22

Index 23

Carers' and teachers' notes 24

How does it grow?

The sunflower grows from a seed. Inside this seed is a tiny plant. The seed also contains food that the tiny plant needs to help it grow.

The sunflower seed starts to grow, or **germinate**, in the spring when the weather is warm and the soil is damp. After a few days, a root pushes its way out of the seed.

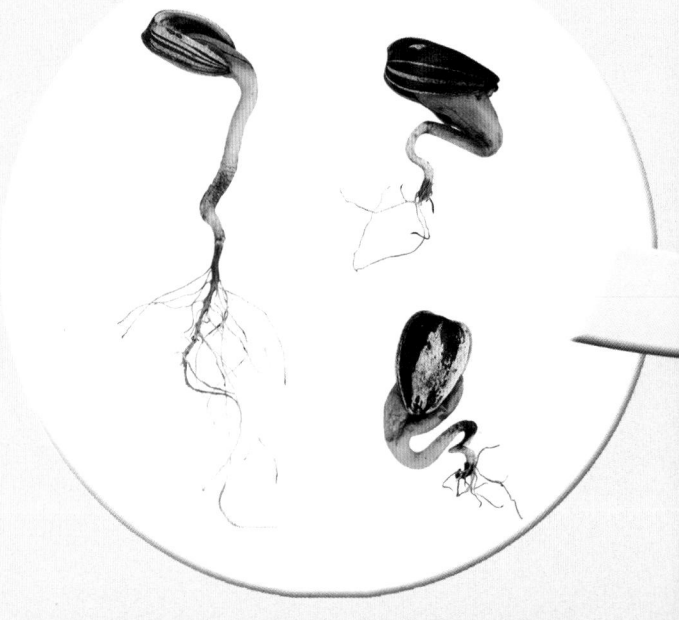

The root grows down into the ground and holds the new plant in the soil.

The root takes water and **minerals** from the soil.

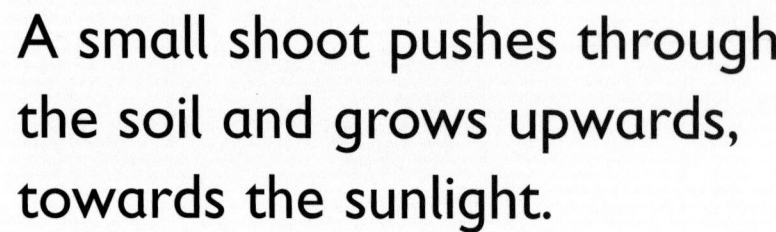

A small shoot pushes through the soil and grows upwards, towards the sunlight.

The little plant is now called a seedling.

Then, the stem starts to grow.

6

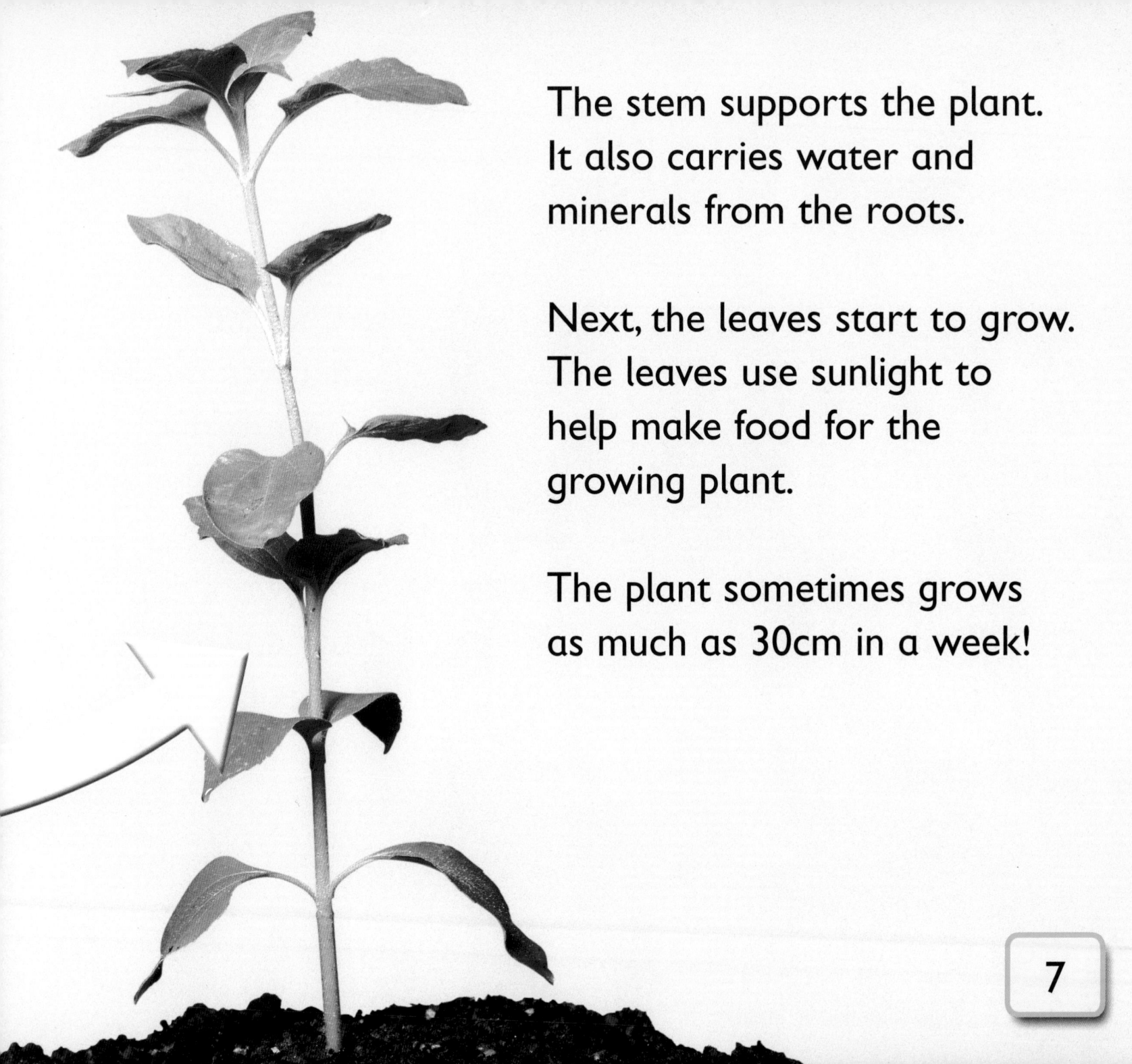

The stem supports the plant. It also carries water and minerals from the roots.

Next, the leaves start to grow. The leaves use sunlight to help make food for the growing plant.

The plant sometimes grows as much as 30cm in a week!

Sunflower sizes

To grow big and strong, the sunflower needs air, water and lots of sunshine.

Sunflowers can grow up to three metres tall. This is one and a half times as tall as a very tall person!

8

Sunflower plants are fully grown
after about three months.

Flowers in bloom

The sunflower plant makes flowers.
What looks like a large flower is
really many small flowers.

The flowers
in the middle
are like
short tubes.

The tube-like
flowers at
the edge
each have a
yellow **petal**.

10

The sunflower needs
a lot of sunshine.

The head of the
sunflower turns
to face the sun all
through the day.

Sunflower seeds

12

Sunflower seeds come from the flowers.

As the flowers die, the petals fall off. But a seed begins to grow inside each flower.

You can see the new seeds when the flower goes brown, after the petals have fallen off.

Growing again

The seeds fall to the ground.

They lie on the ground until
the following spring.

Then, when the earth is warm
and **moist**, the seeds germinate
and start to grow again.

Good to eat

Sunflower seeds are used for food.

They are very good for you. They help you to grow strong and healthy.

Roasted seeds make a delicious snack!

Sunflower oil is made from the sunflower seeds. It is used in cooking and in salads.

How to grow a sunflower

What you need:
- Sunflower seeds
- Compost
- 10cm pots

What to do:

Fill the pots with moist compost.

Make two holes in the compost, 2 or 3cm deep.

Drop a seed into each hole and cover them over with moist compost.

Place the pots in a warm room and keep the compost moist, but not wet.

After a few days the seedlings will start to grow!

Planting the seedlings

Make holes, about 30cm apart, in the soil.

Turn the pots upside down and gently tip out the seedlings.

Drop the seedlings into the holes.

Make sure that you press the soil down firmly around the roots.

Water the seedlings at least once a week if the weather is dry.

Watch your sunflower plants grow!

Glossary

Germinate – when a seed starts to grow and develop.

Minerals – substances that plants take up from the soil with their roots and use to help them grow.

Moist – slightly damp.

Petal – the parts of a flower that are often brightly coloured.

Index

compost 18, 19

flowers 10–11, 13

food
  for people 16
  for plants 4, 5, 7

germinate 4, 15, 22

leaves 7

minerals 5, 7, 22

moist compost/
  earth 15, 18, 19, 22

petals 10, 13, 22

plants
  how they grow
  4–7, 8, 15
  how to grow
  18–19
  planting seedling
  20–21

roots 4, 5

seedlings 6, 19, 20–1

seeds
  eating 16
  germination 4, 15
  new 13, 15
  planting 18–19

size of plants 7, 8, 9

stem 6, 7

sunlight 7, 8, 11

Carers' and teachers' notes

- Explain that this book is non-fiction and that it has a contents page, a glossary and an index.
- Explain the purpose of the index (to locate information) and the glossary (to explain difficult or specialist words in the text).
- Talk about the name of the flower and its link with the sun.
- Explain that most of the book is about how a sunflower grows, and that the last four pages give simple instructions for growing your own sunflower.
- Explain the word 'seed' as the very beginning of a flower's life. Emphasize that air, water and warmth are essential to make the tiny plant grow.
- Draw a picture of a sunflower and label its parts – root, stem, leaves, flower and petals.
- Explain that all living things grow and that the plant grows just as children grow – but a lot faster!
- After reading through pages 6–7 together, find out what 30cm looks like, using a ruler.

- Look at the photograph of the sunflower on page 10. How many petals can your child count? What colour are the petals?
- Show the inside of an apple to your child, and explain that the pips are a type of seed. Warn your child that not all seeds are good to eat like those of the sunflower.
- Look at the word 'sunflower'. Count the number of times the word 'sunflower' appears in the book.
- Together, follow the step-by-step instructions for growing a sunflower.
- Hold a competition for your child and his/her friends to see whose sunflower grows the tallest.
- Grow another fast-growing plant from seed, e.g. a runner bean, or some cress. Together, note down each stage of the plant's development under the heading 'How does it grow?'
- Help your child to write a set of instructions explaining how to grow the new plant.